THE KILLIN BRANCH RAILWAY

By

Colin Hogarth

STIRLING DISTRICT LIBRARIES

ISBN 1 870542 24 X

Published by
Stirling District Libraries
Stirling

Printed by
Cordfall Ltd
041 332 4640

Contents

~1~
BEFORE THE IRON HORSE

One of the more interesting and eccentric features of the British character is the love for lost causes and nowhere is this more evident than in the struggling railway history of Scotland's small branch lines. During the Victorian railway revolution, when railway development and construction was at its peak, landowners felt somehow incomplete if they did not have some form of railway running across their estates, as long as it wasn't within sight of their conservatories!

One such landowner was the Marquis of Breadalbane, a wealthy but rather eccentric chap who, some may say, had far more money than sense. His Highland estate, called Breadalbane, covered a band of land stretching right across Scotland from Oban in the west to Aberfeldy and beyond in the east. It included many thousands of acres of prime grazing land around the shores of Loch Tay, and as many acres again of fertile farmland in Strath Fillan. He also owned huge tracts of moorland, including Rannoch Moor as well as much of Scotland's finest mountain scenery.

Nestled amongst this were towns and villages such as Crianlarich, Bridge of Orchy, Kenmore and the popular tourist village at the southend of Loch Tay, Killin, which is where our story starts.

Killin originally grew up around a medieval church and the name itself is derived from the Gaelic meaning "white church". However in the years we are concerned with it survived as a farming town, acting as a market for the many hill sheep farmers who grazed their animals on the shores of Loch Tay.

Each month local farmers would gather their flocks and drive the herds down the hills to Killin. Once they had reached the village they would hope to get a fair price for their beasts which would then allow them to buy whatever they needed in the village before retiring to a local ale house for the afternoon. This helped boost the village economy no end and in no time at all a reasonable number of shops, public houses and other useful services had sprung up.

The village also acted as an overnight stopping point for the long distance cattle and sheep drovers travelling from as far away as Skye and the Western Isles to the annual markets held in Perth and Falkirk. The villagers did their best to accommodate these weary walkers and in time the existing inns expanded and, more importantly, blacksmiths set up their forges in the village.

However, despite the fact that Killin had become the Watford Gap of the Highlands, communications in the area were still very poor. The roads leading into, and out of, the village were little more than dirt tracks, a situation which was more or less the same right across Scotland. This is where railways enter the scene. Cars had not been invented, as yet, and the only available road transport was the faithful horse and cart which, even at the

Former station at the top of Glenogle.

best of times, and on the best of roads, was neither efficient nor comfortable.

Travellers were demanding more than dirt tracks and battered bodies and by 1870, probably much to the relief of the local horse population among others, the first rails began to penetrate into the glens. Killin's first glimpse of the 'iron horse' was the Callander to Oban railway line which reached the head of nearby Glenogle in 1870. Three years later it was completed as far as Tyndrum and soon after its destination on the west coast, Oban was reached. At its nearest point, the new railway was just over five miles from Killin and a station, called Killin Station, was opened at the head of Glenogle. In order to use their new station the villagers had to mount up on horse back, ride five miles across the hillsides and moorland only to find that on arrival, there was no where to 'park' their beasts.

On the other hand, the new transport system was a godsend for the travelling drovers. It meant they could take the boat to Oban, load their animals on to the train and travel to Callander in far less time than before. From there it was just a matter of changing trains for Perth. Good news for the drover but the villagers of Killin were far from happy. Now that the journey could be done in less than a day there was no need for the cattle men to stop in Killin and, as a result, less business for the inns, shops and blacksmiths.

Killin's predicament was made even worse when the Highland Railway Company opened their railway between Perth and Inverness. This was soon followed by a branch line to the town of Aberfeldy at the north end of Loch Tay. Now the local sheep farmers were heading from the shores of Loch Tay to Aberfeldy where they could take the train to Perth. Meanwhile poor little Killin was sitting like a child in a dentist's waiting room, not particularly happy and rather worried.

Business was going down hill faster than a shepherd in a thunder storm. Farmers had no need to pass through the village and so they didn't. The local market continued but something had to be done to put Killin back on the map. In these Victorian days of railway travel a town or village in the Highlands could easily slip into oblivion if it did not possess a railway station.

In 1881 the Marquis noticed the potential that the village of Killin held as a possible tourist attraction or even as a Highland holiday resort. Health spas and resorts were all the rage elsewhere in the country, all he had to do was guide the blinkered Victorians to it. In his infinite wisdom he hit upon the idea of opening a short branch line between the shores of Loch Tay and the station at the head of Glenogle. This way the village would be directly connected into Britain's main railway network. People could travel from far and wide to experience the joys of Loch Tay, Killin and the surrounding country, in fact all the land that he owned.

He had soon convinced himself that the need for a railway was great. In addition to bringing tourists to the area he could also persuade local shopkeepers, farmers and even villagers to travel on it or use it for the transportation of their supplies. So without any more ado he set about conceiving his brainchild.

His first move was to ask the Callander & Oban Railway Company if they would build and operate such a line. However his proposals fell on deaf ears and after much arguing, mainly on his part, he was politely shown the door. Unabashed he left their offices and headed for the Caledonian Railway Company who were next to see his plans. The C.R. operated the Callander & Oban Railway and the Marquis thought they would he fair game. They too, however, refused to build the apparently stillborn line but did agree to operate it if it were built by someone else. Perhaps this acted as a spur to the man who was not used to admitting defeat. If nobody else would build his line, then he would jolly well do it himself!

After wasting so much time in vain he left it not a second longer before calling a meeting in the Killin Drill Hall where he divulged his plans to the local people. On the night of October 19, 1882, a large crowd made up of people ranging from local hill shepherds to wealthy businessmen had gathered in the packed village hall. The Marquis took the floor and was soon briefing the assembled population with the facts, figures and personal opinions about this exciting new project. Not surprisingly the gathering were somewhat taken aback by the man's proposals which he had packaged up and presented before them in order to persuade them that it was in their best interests to have this new railway. The question on most lips however was, where would the necessary funds come from?

Clapping his hands, the Marquis introduced the isolated community to the world of stocks and shares and that by buying shares in the new railway the local people could own it, and even make some money in the process. So with the backing of his faithful villagers he set about the task of finding out how much the railway would cost to build.

Tenders were submitted to the newly formed Killin Railway Company by construction firms from all over Scotland. They ranged from the most expensive at £22,442 to the cheapest at £13,783.

	£	s	d
Braddock & Mathews, Airdrie.	22,442	6	3
D. Manuel, Glasgow.	20,487	6	6
Henderson, Mathew & Co.	20,277	0	2
A & H Boyle, Hamilton.	19,136	12	2
David Shank, Bothwell.	17,932	0	0
Scott & Best, Leith.	17,638	8	6
N.I. Adams, Cullen.	16,918	2	11
Hugh Kennedy & Son, Patrick.	16,796	19	2
A & K MacDonald, Skye.	13,783	8	0

The railway company considered all the tenders very carefully and finally decided to plump for the cheapest. This was submitted by a company from Skye called A & K MacDonald whose estimated cost was considerably lower than any of the other companies. Once a cost had been sorted out the Marquis had share certificates drawn up and trading in the new company began. Each share cost £1 and for every share bought by the local villagers the Marquis pledged to buy another himself. In short he would end up owning half the shares and would have complete control over the company. After the Marquis, with a share value of £2015, the Callander & Oban Railway Company had the next largest handful of shares with 1200. After this the remaining shares were bought by local business men, shopkeepers, villagers and even lowly shepherds.

The share issue also decided who were going to be the new company's new board of directors. The Marquis took up position as chairman of the Killin Railway Company with four joint directors appointed below him. As the minimum share value for a directorship was £200 only four men qualified for such a position. They were Mr Charles Stewart, of Killin, who became deputy chairman, Sir Donald Currie who invested £1000 in the railway, Mr John Willison and Mr John Cameron. The company's secretary was Mr Robert Robertson who was banker with the Bank of Scotland in Killin. Although the C & O had no director on the branch line board, they did have a powerful say in the company's affairs.

After finding a company to build the new railway the Marquis needed a good engineer to plan its route and overlook construction. This he found in the form of John Strain an excellent engineer who had been responsible for much of the Callander to Oban railway line. Strain surveyed the land and estimated the line's total cost would be somewhere in the region of £28,552 including stations, bridges and his fee. By the time that the first shareholders' meeting was due the company's income could be summarised as follows:

Cash	£ 8,200
Shares for value of land	£ 2,726
Shares for value of sleepers	£ 1,210
Shares for value of rails	£ 3,465
Money raised by loans	£ 5,200
TOTAL	£20,801

Even including a generous loan from Robertson's bank, the total was still £7,751 short of Strain's estimated cost and still too low to allow construction to get under way. So the Marquis decided that as well as his hefty financial support and his donation of land on which the line would be built he would also supply enough rails and sleepers to build it with. With this the Marquis confidently predicted that his wee railway would be open and running for the summer traffic of 1885.

~ 2 ~

PLANNING AND CONSTRUCTION

MacDonald began work in the summer of 1883 and planned to hand over the railway two years later. Few physical barriers existed and, as the land between Killin and Glenoglehead was remarkably even in terrain, only minimum earthworks were needed. The formation of the trackbed between Killin Junction and Killin involved the removal of 100,000 cubic yards of earth but between Killin and Loch Tay no earthworks were needed at all as the trackbed ran out on to the flat flood plain. However, despite this, construction was not all plain sailing. Money was tight even at the best of times and at one point there were even plans to abandon building the line between Killin and because of the cost involved. As Loch Tay was intended to be one of the line's main attractions, and as the Marquis intended to connect up a steam boat service, he was adamant that it should be included in the plans. To save money, the company considered bringing the steam boats up the River Lochay to the Killin Hotel where they could join with the railway. This, it was decided, would cost just as much as the river would have to be canalised before any attempt was made to bring boats in.

Cattle culvert under Callander & Oban line at Killin Junction, 1991

BR 2-6-4 crosses Dochart Viaduct

So Loch Tay was to stay, but money was still scarce. When MacDonald had estimated the cost of building the line he had banked on building a metal girder bridge across the River Dochart. However Strain insisted on a costly five arch stone viaduct, adding an extra £1000 on to MacDonald's bill. The railway company agreed to Strain's plans and so MacDonald had to consent but where he was to find the necessary funds was to be a problem. As it was he had far underestimated the cost of building the railway and he was slowly slipping into financial ruin. The Killin Railway Company were no help either. They too had little money and could not afford to help. So MacDonald slipped into a sea of unpaid bills and finally bankruptcy, leaving the little railway company to foot the bill.

When Strain inspected the line in August 1884 he was disappointed with the lack of progress. Only the piers of the Dochart viaduct had been built and there was little sign of the concrete work which had to be completed before the winter's first frosts which were expected within two months. The cement for the concrete had not even arrived and it was soon found out that no one would deal with MacDonald without a financial guarantee from the railway directors. This was duly made and 50 tons of concrete were sent up by train from J.C. Johnson & Co. of the Gateshead Cement Works.

MacDonald was still sure that he would complete the job in time but he had badly underestimated the cost of the line and by November 1884 his funds were arrested by creditors and the contract to build the line was terminated. An angry bunch of unpaid navvies descended on the railway company's offices but they too could not afford to pay the wages.

Without the pay due to them, the strong band of men refused to leave the area until Strain stepped in and guaranteed their wages. Work continued but once they had received their money, many of the men left the line like rats off a sinking ship. There was no shortage of similar work elsewhere and good navvies had little difficulty in finding alternative employment.

Even buying fodder for horses was a problem and no one would deal with the company without the guarantee of the Marquis. Meanwhile Strain was becoming more and more angry at the way the whole business was being run. Construction ceased and Strain found himself in the centre of chaos, left to sort the whole affair out. He was frank about what he thought of the Killin Railway Company and their disorganised administrative affairs and told them so. In a long letter he told the directors that they had got what they deserved by accepting the lowest tender and that the board was morally wrong for letting the navvies wages fall into arrears. In total the Killin directors had paid out over £10,316 to MacDonald who, according to Strain, had done a great deal of work well and very cheaply.

After terminating MacDonald's contract Strain contacted a Glasgow firm, under John Best, who were hired to finish the work. Best restarted construction late in the year but poor weather conditions and a shortage of labour hindered further progress. By 1885, 73% of the earthworks had been completed and 84% of the bridges, cattle creeps and culverts were finished. However, no sooner had they overcome one problem than another reared its ugly head.

This time it was the C & O. A junction with the Callander to Oban railway at Glenoglehead had previously been planned at a cost of £2,000 but the C & O later decided that a more expensive layout, costing at least £4,500, was required and insisted that the Killin Railway Company foot the bill. This they could not do so a bitter argument between the mighty C & O and the comparatively insignificant branch company ensued. The outcome was that if the Killin directors didn't pay for the necessary junction then they could forget about any connection with the C & O. So the Marquis stepped in and paid up. The new, and extremely expensive, plans were reluctantly accepted by the railway's poverty stricken directors and the necessary rail was ordered. From Glasgow the track was carried by ship up to Oban where it was then loaded on to a Caley train and taken along the C & O to Glenoglehead Station. On arrival it was discovered that no points had been bought and seventy-two 24ft sections of rail were sent to the General Railway and Electrical Appliance Company in Glasgow where they were fashioned into points and crossovers.

The Marquis of Breadalbane's predictions of opening the new line for the summer of 1885 seemed somewhat optimistic as the summer approached and the line was far from complete. The days dragged on and the line slowly began to take shape. Further bank loans were taken out and the Marquis continued to delve deeper into his seemingly bottomless pockets in order to turn his dream into reality.

Bridge over River Lochay, 1991

Killin Junction Station Cottages, 1991

~ 3 ~

CROSSING THE DOCHART AND LOCHAY

One of the line's biggest challenges and most ambitious projects was the five arch concrete viaduct built over the raging waters of the River Dochart. Stretching for a total of 103 yards and standing 38ft above the turbulent waters it was a major construction task. In the late 19th century concrete was a fairly new construction material and engineers all over the country were keen to experiment with the new medium. The Dochart was just one of many concrete bridges to pop up across Highland rivers and gorges. It took months to complete, with workmen carefully applying layers of concrete and then giving each one several days to dry before adding the next. Poor weather could be relied on to hinder this slow process but once finished it was a structure that its creators could be truly proud of. When it was inspected by the Board of Trade it took them at least twenty minutes to drill just one inch into the concrete. This created much humour amongst the local people and gave the inspectors some cause for embarrassment.

The only other bridge of any notable size on the railway was the less spectacular eight-span oregon pine structure which crossed the River Lochay, less than a mile down the track from the Dochart Viaduct. Measuring 54 yards in length, it was originally made up of eight spans measuring just two feet each. The piles, driven 40 ft into the river bed, were made of larch with the track deck, running 27ft above the water level, built from pitch pine. However in later years this was replaced with a three span metal girder bridge mounted on concrete supports.

Once completed the single track line ran for a little over five and a quarter miles. A total of three stations, including Killin Junction, were built and an additional siding was installed at Acharn farm, midway between Killin and Killin Junction. The track gauge was a standard 4ft 8in and the permanent way was laid with 60lb Vignalles steel rails, divided into 24ft lengths. This was laid on uncreosoted Riga redwood sleepers and ballasted with broken whinstone and gravel.

As the railway's route took it through predominantly open grazing land it had to be fenced in to avoid animals straying onto the tracks. This was done mainly with wire and post fences and gates and cattle creeps were supplied at points along the line's course. A total of nine culverts and underbridges were supplied for cattle and roads and a further four were built across burns and rivers. All were stone built with masonry abutments. Despite the many underpasses, the railway it had only one overbridge, crossing the line's deepest cutting, just outside Killin village. This had a span of 15 feet and the timber deck was mounted on masonry abutments.

~ 4 ~

KILLIN JUNCTION STATION

The little railway had a total of three passenger stations. The first to be encountered by most rail travellers was the mighty Killin Junction. Perched at the summit of Scotland's darkest glen, Glenogle, it was built specifically as a changeover point between the C & O railway and the Killin branch. By rail it was 60 miles from Edinburgh and 51 miles east of Oban. No settlement existed near the junction and the nearest hamlet with a station was Luib, a couple of miles west. It was quite strictly defined only as an interchange point and the C & O often got quite angry when it was used as anything else. For this reason access to the station was made as difficult as possible. No roads were supplied to the station and thick forestry was later planted around it. This caused something of a problem for those living near Killin Junction who had expected to be allowed to use the new junction station when the original one at Glenoglehead closed. However on contacting the C & O with their query, they were told it served only as an interchange platform.

The station itself consisted of two platforms. One was an island platform between the C & O and the Killin branch and the other a down platform located to the south of the island platform. No footbridge was originally built connecting the up and down platforms and passengers had to cross the tracks at either end

of the platforms. The wooden station building was built on the up-island platform. It was constructed of tongued and grooved timber mounted on a concrete base which was set into the platform. As heat inside was derived from coal and wood fires three brick chimneys were built, one at either end and one in the middle of the grey slate roof. The exterior wood was painted in a plain cream livery with the doors, bargeboards, window frames, gutters and downpipes painted in blue-grey. Inside, the building contained a waiting room cum booking hall, a ladies' waiting room, staff room and stationmaster's office and toilets. Mounted on the down platform was a smaller wooden shed of similar basic design and livery.

To the east of the station, where the tracks split off to Glenogle and Killin, a red brick signal box was built and payed for by the Killin Railway Company. Known as the East box, it contained 26 levers and also operated the tablet apparatus for the mainline. A smaller 22 frame box was supplied by the C & O at the west end of the station. The majority of the trackwork at the junction was controlled from a nine-lever open ground frame at the east end of the island platform. However an electrically operated turnout, controlling the western end of the passing loop, was fitted as was a catch point in the up platform line which was designed to derail runaways descending the grade. All the semaphore signals at the junction were mounted on lattice posts. The down main advance up and starter main home was track circuited as it was obscured from sight from the signal cabin by the adjacent cutting. This triple-armed signal, like the down main starter, branch starter and the calling arm at the western end of the branch platform, was an upper-quadrant. The up main distant, up main starter and branch advanced starter were all lower-quadrant; the down main distant and branch distant were fixed.

The junction had no goods yard but the longer of the two branch sidings was often used for the storage or unloading of goods wagons. The shorter siding was usually all that was necessary to accommodate the Killin train and its stock. A goods shed, which had originally stood at the former Killin Station and had been blown down in a gale, was re-erected at the junction at no cost to the Killin company.

The junction station had been by far the most expensive part of the new branch to build. In total the track layout had cost £4,500 and in addition to this the Killin Railway Co. paid £480 for the buildings, platforms and fittings and a further £400 for a signalling system. Still without the junction the line would have had little point in operating and no destination in life.

Camping Coach at Killin yard.

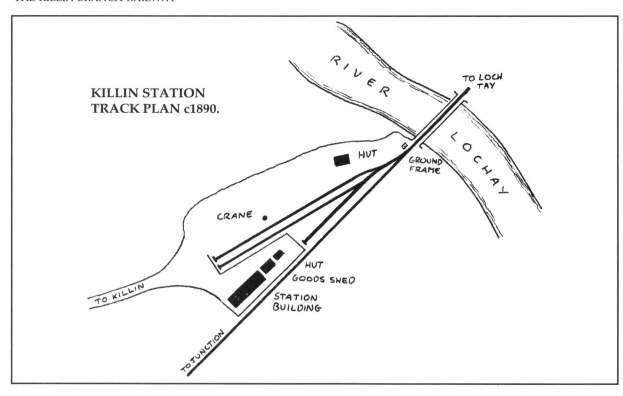

KILLIN STATION TRACK PLAN c1890.

RIVER

LOCHAY

TO LOCH TAY

HUT

GROUND FRAME

CRANE

TO KILLIN

HUT GOODS SHED

STATION BUILDING

TO JUNCTION

Mess Hut at Loch Tay, now a shed, 1991.

~ 5 ~

KILLIN STATION

The four miles of single track between Killin Junction and Killin station took the railway down through open moorland and deciduous woodland before it reached the outskirts of the village of Killin. About a mile west of Killin a short single line siding was built around 1900 to serve Acharn Farm. The siding, which was accessible by a two-lever open ground frame opened using a key held on the single line tablet, was to allow the farm to load sheep, bound for Killin market. Before reaching Killin Station the railway had to skirt along the back of the village on a small embankment, cross the mighty Dochart viaduct and continue along behind the houses before reaching its destination.

Killin Station was located just yards from the centre of Killin on the banks of the River Lochay. It had a single concrete platform on which sat the station building, a small brick goods shed and a wooden hut. The station building was of wooden construction and bore little similarity to its big brother at Killin Junction. The platform was reached from the car park through a short open hallway which split the building in two. On one side it contained the stationmaster's office, a ticket office and a store room and on the other a waiting room, a ladies' room and a gents toilet accessible from the outside. To the east of the station building there was a small red brick goods shed sharing the platform. It had a sliding door on both platform and car park side and was used for small items such as parcels, groceries etc. Beside this was a small wooden hut used by staff as a mess room and for storing lamps and other railway accessories.

Behind the station was a small goods yard consisting of three sidings, a short one which terminated at the platform end and two longer ones which ran on behind the station. Originally the railway directors had hoped to acquire the small yard crane from the previous Killin Station for the siding but the C & O decided they wished to keep it and duly dispatched it to Connel Ferry. A new crane was purchased from Buttars of Glasgow at a cost of £53 8s. The cast iron lever frame which operated the siding points was kept locked with the key to this fixed on the single line tablet stored in the engine's cab.

In the village of Killin two semi-detached houses were built for the stationmaster and the station's porter-guard. These were built at the edge of the village at a cost of £270 and were rented out to the staff at ls 9d per week each. The total cost of Killin Station, including the goods shed and all fittings, but excluding the cost of track, was about £320.

~ 6 ~

LOCH TAY STATION

Between Killin and Loch Tay Station, the terminus of the line, the track ran across the Lochay bridge before continuing over the relatively flat glacial deposits at the head of Loch Tay. A mile from Killin the railway reached the shores of Loch Tay and perched on the waterside was Loch Tay Station. Loch Tay was the jewel in the Breadalbane Estate's crown. Along with Breadalbane's plans for the Killin railway he was also in the midst of starting a regular steamboat service on the waters of Loch Tay.

As there was no village or settlement of any nature near Loch Tay Station its prime purpose was to serve the boats on the loch and to enable boats to load or unload at the station a timber pier, complete with a set of rails, was projected out into the waters. Between the loch and the station building a set of short sidings and a goods yard was built to serve both the railway and steamships. Both the pier line and the sidings joined on to the main branch just west of the station and a locked seven-lever ground

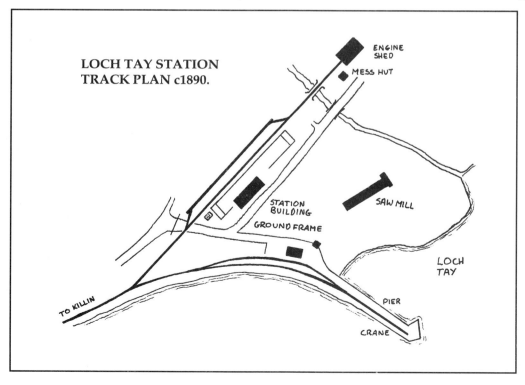

LOCH TAY STATION
TRACK PLAN c1890.

ENGINE SHED
MESS HUT
STATION BUILDING
GROUND FRAME
SAW MILL
LOCH TAY
TO KILLIN
PIER
CRANE

frame, mounted on a four foot high wooden platform accessible by a set of steps, operated the points. Three of the levers operated the runaround loop and the other four controlled the sidings and pier railway.

The station itself consisted of a single platform, long enough to accommodate two coaches, built on the south side of the tracks. On the platform was a small wooden building similar to that at Killin. Inside there was a waiting room, a partitioned ladies room, a ticket office and a gents toilet. It was painted in gamboge white with a tarpaulin roof. Doors, downpipes, window frames and the single chimney were of a maroon livery. The platform was wooden with a gravel surface which in later years became home to two caravans. A short distance further east a small wooden engine shed was built into the steep hillside. It was constructed of slatted wood and contained an engine pit for locomotive maintenance. Beside the shed a small mess room was supplied for use by the driver and fireman who would take their tea break while the engine drank at the metal water column fed by a nearby stream.

The station and instruments had cost a total of £250 and the engine shed a further £120. A pair of cottages was also supplied for use by the train crew and their families. To ensure communication between the three stations a railway telephone system was installed at a cost of £140. The cables for this ran alongside the track.

Loch Tay Station, present day.

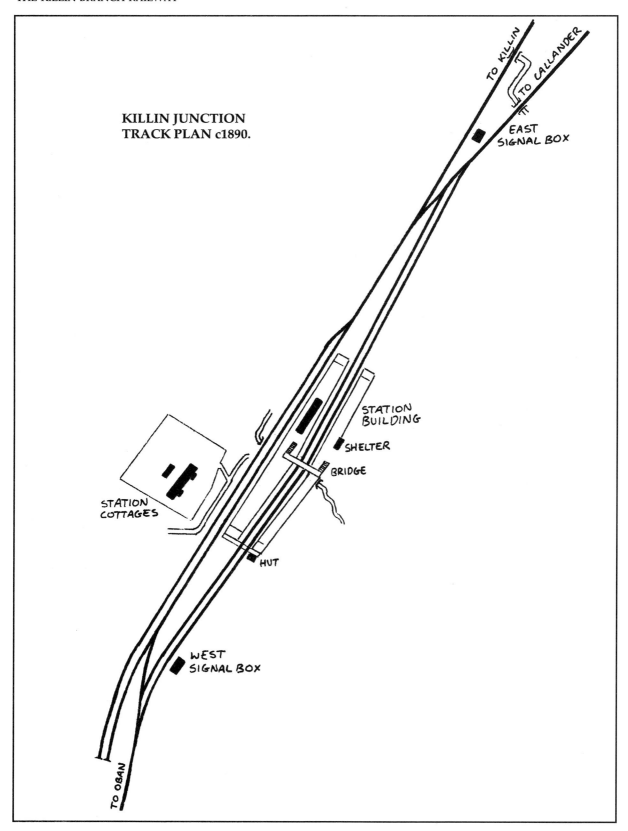

**KILLIN JUNCTION
TRACK PLAN c1890.**

TO KILLIN

TO CALLANDER

EAST
SIGNAL BOX

STATION
BUILDING

SHELTER

BRIDGE

STATION
COTTAGES

HUT

WEST
SIGNAL BOX

TO OBAN

~ 7 ~

FINAL TOUCHES

Once the main track and stations were completed it was time to fit the railway out with all the instruments, furniture and fittings which were necessary for its everyday running. This job fell to Robertson as company secretary. After consulting the C & O with regards to what he needed he ordered the necessary ticket machines and office furniture from a Glasgow company. They were duly sent and Robertson ordered another company to print tickets and timetables. As only one engine would be running on the line at any one time no tablet apparatus was needed and railway signalling could be kept to a bare minimum. The biggest, and probably most trivial cause for debate was the naming of the stations. The first suggestions for the three little railway outposts were Killin Junction, Killin and Killin Pier. However the Marquis was unhappy about the overuse of Killin in this choice and the lack of reference to Loch Tay. It was his opinion, and part of his

business strategy, that it would be the loch which would draw tourists to the area and so some reference had to be made in the titles. Accordingly the names were changed to Killin Junction, Killin and Killin Pier-Loch Tay. However for much of its life the terminus at Loch Tay just became known as Loch Tay Station.

Signs were ordered by the directors and these soon arrived. However when Robertson took delivery of the new boards he noticed one just read 'Junction'. Worrying that some dreadful omission had been made he hastily contacted the directors and it was explained that to save money they were going to acquire the sign from Killin Station, at the head of Glenogle, when it closed and join the two together. On the opening of the Killin Branch the old C & O Killin Station, just south of Killin Junction, was renamed Glenoglehead.

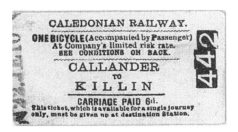

Single coach branch train gets up steam at Killin Junction.

Killin branch train at Loch Tay, 28.7.31.

~ 8 ~

ALL READY

By the end of 1885, once everything was completed and the railway had been kitted out to the best of the company's ability and low budget, Robertson wrote to the Board of Trade to set a date for the line's inspection. A prompt reply soon found its way into the Highlands and Major Marindin, the assistant secretary of the railway department, was expected for the inspection on January 28, 1886. On the day a special train was laid on at the junction to meet the Major and his party who were expected on the C & O railway that evening. However luck was against the little railway once again and a fierce snowstorm swept down the glen, blotting the new tracks from sight under a deep white carpet. Robertson was forced to inform the Board of Trade, the inspection was cancelled and the railway had to remain closed until the snow had melted and a full inspection could be carried out.

However for the local folk the sudden snowstorm had caused something of a problem. The sudden change in weather conditions had taken everyone quite by surprise and many were without any form of winter fuel to help take the chill off their cold houses. As they sat freezing in their snowcapped village houses over 140 tons of coal awaited them at Killin Junction station. As the snow had blocked the roads and made them impassable, the people appealed to the railway company to do something about the situation. In turn the railway directors pleaded with the Board of Trade who consented and allowed the mission of mercy to go ahead. The gleaming blue Caley engine, snug in its shed, set out into the winter sunshine and, after a short time, returned from the junction, slightly dirtier but none the less very welcome with its load of winter fuel. However it didn't end there. On seeing this the local farmers were next to ask a favour of the little railway. They too had not been expecting such a fierce storm quite so early on and their sheep and cattle were dying in the fields for want of hay. Again the little engine came to the rescue and soon a brisk trade in hay ensued.

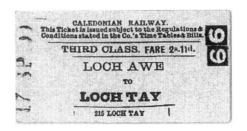

~ 9 ~

BOARD OF TRADE INSPECTION

Eventually, a month later in February, Major Marindin and his party of engineers made their way into the Highlands to the line and began the inspection. After a thorough inspection of the trackwork, bridges, earthworks and the three stations the major was happy with what he saw and allowed operation to begin, provided a list of seven points was noted and seen to by the railway directors. These were as follows.

1) Check rail to be fitted on 10 chain curve.
2) At Killin and Loch Tay stations the general waiting room has to be partitioned off for a ladies' waiting room.
3) Stops to be fitted on some of the field gates to prevent them from opening onto the line.
4) A little (more) ballast is required in places.
5) Only one engine to be in steam, or two coupled together, shall be allowed on the line at any one time.
6) Maximum speed 20mph.
7) Chimney must be in front when running on the falling gradient from the Junction to Killin.

He also recommended that the Dochart viaduct be regularly inspected, at least every three months for any signs of wear and tear.

On seeing the list of improvements and recommendations the railway directors breathed a sigh of relief that nothing major was out of place as it was doubtful if there was any money left in the company funds for any repairs or further construction. Before the major headed back for Edinburgh aboard a special train, he told the gathering of directors and shareholders, "I can recommend that the opening of the Killin Railway for passenger traffic may be sanctioned."

With this news the people of Killin cheered and those that had made the whole venture possible patted each other on the back before going off to celebrate. The Marquis of Breadalbane's dream had now become a reality but a tough and testing time lay ahead for the little Highland railway. It was destined to become very much part of village life for the local people but at the same time it was never very far away from suffering at the hands of the harsh business world.

~ 10 ~
OPENING CEREMONY

Picture the scene. The gleaming metal rails of a small Highland railway meandering down through open moorland and deciduous woodland, and then running on until it meets with the clean blue waters of a graceful Scottish loch, bounded on all sides by magnificent mountains and crowned by the slow setting late evening sun. What could possibly have been more pleasant on a warm summers evening than a short train journey behind a smart blue engine through acres of beautiful countryside before relaxing on the timber decks of a fine oak built vessel, sipping a whisky and watching the red of the sun slowly melt over the high hills? It all sounds truly idyllic, like a scene conjured up by some famous novelist writing whilst on safari or exploring the foot hills of Kenya. However this paradise could be sampled nearer to home and in the more humble territory of the Scottish Highlands.

The Marquis and his villagers had finally managed to make their dream come true. After all the hard work, poverty and uncertainty the railway had been completed, passed by the

Killin Station

Board of Trade and was now ready for opening. They were going to make sure it was an opening ceremony not to be missed. Although passenger operation was not to begin until after April 1, 1886 the opening ceremony was planned for March 13 and was to be a surprisingly grand affair for such a small railway company. Invitations were sent out far and wide, reaching railway officials and important people the length and breadth of Scotland. To the surprise of the railway directors many of the senior railwaymen and civic dignitaries who were sent invitations actually accepted them. Among them were John Strain, the line's engineer and the Highland Railway supervisor and locomotive designer David Jones. One would have thought after all the difficulties Strain had with the company and all the harsh words that were swapped he may have been glad to see the back of them.

When the day arrived, and the sun decided to bless the line, the celebrations began. A special train, boarded by a host of celebrities, was laid on at Callander Station. After toiling up the steep line through Glenogle, it began its journey down the new stretch of railway at Killin Junction. After descending to Killin Station, the wee train, hauled by the specially polished Killin Pug, ran on through to Loch Tay Station where the gathering were guided on to a steamboat and treated to a cruise around Loch Tay.

After an exhilarating boat journey, the assembled party returned to Loch Tay Station where the guests disembarked and reboarded the awaiting train. It ran back up the line to Killin where tables had been set out in the park for luncheon. The guests sat down to the prepared feast but before the eating began the traditional opening speeches had to be delivered. The Marquis was first, followed by Strain who claimed that the Dochart viaduct was the most ambitious work he had ever attempted in mass concrete whereupon Best said the success of the line had already proved itself and he was working on a similar project in Spain, using the Killin branch as a model.

Breadalbane's dream was now reality but the railway's future was not to be as rosy as those at the opening lunch optimistically predicted. The tough gradient between Killin and Killin junction was not to be the only uphill struggle the line's trains would face. However whatever befell the little line it would always be close to the hearts of the local people who had fought for its opening and would continue to battle to retain it.

LMS No. 15103 (formerly CR 1177) mainstay of the branch from 1889 into 1940s.

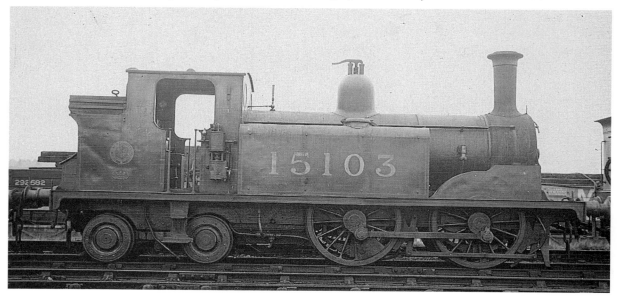

~ 11 ~

EARLY DAYS

The first year of operation had shown a good result for the little railway which had suffered so much in its conception from financial worries and lack of funds. However even with a small profit standing proud from the jumbled figures in the hurriedly scrawled company accounts, the directors could not just sit back and let the railway look after itself. It was soon discovered that it needed constant attention and promoting to make it pay. With Breadalbane's power and authority over the local community he was the very man to set about marketing its values among the villagers and traders.

As many of the local shopkeepers and village merchants held shares in the railway it was obvious that they would want to make the best use of the line for delivery of goods from the outside world. The weekly provisions would arrive in hampers from Glasgow on the Callander to Oban line and be transferred on to the wee train at Killin Junction. However the smooth, organised transfer machine, namely the station porter, would often become engrossed in other business to the cost of the village shopkeepers. On many occasions when wealthy travellers, loaded down with a large assortment of jumbled luggage, arrived at the junction, the porter found it quite a bit more lucrative to help them with their belongings in exchange for the odd 'bit o' silver' rather than offload the heavy hampers. This often resulted in an irate Killin merchant being told that his

fresh morning bread, or weekly stock, had been carried off to Oban!

Along with supplies, the village mail and parcels were also brought in by train, as was common at that time, and to supplement the railway company's income it was suggested that the directors organise a village parcel delivery service. However the Marquis was not keen on the plan, on the grounds that a second porter would be required to deliver the packages. He later relented and the village parcels service began, with the following scale of charges.

Under 14lbs	1d
15lbs - 28lbs	2d
29lbs - 36lbs	3d
37lbs - 112lbs	4d

~ 12 ~

SHEEP TRAFFIC

With the Killin cattle and sheep auction sited just yards from the village station, farmers from the outlying areas, and especially those living near the junction, were encouraged to use the line for the transportation of their beasts to the weekly auctions. On market days, before the introduction of road transport, hill sheep farmers from around Loch Tay would gather their flocks and descend to the piers scattered around the loch's shores where they would await the arrival of either *Carlotta* or *Sybilla*, two of Breadalbane's cargo steamers. As far as transport and local enterprise went, the Marquis had almost every opening tapped with trains and steamships. Once loaded the steamers would ply the waters to the jetty at Loch Tay Station. In the early years of the railway a long wooden pier was projected out into the loch, from Loch Tay Station, where steamers could transfer their cargoes straight on to the awaiting trains. The animals, once safely aboard the Killin bound train, would then be rushed off to market. At the same time train loads of sheep would be winding their way down from the junction and from Acharn farm.

For farmers intent on taking their animals further afield, to the large markets of Perth and Falkirk the easiest, and most direct route was to travel down to Aberfeldy then take the Highland Railway down the Tay Valley right into Perth. The Killin Railway Company, however, planned to change all this and Robertson set about trying to persuade his farming friends and bank clients to reroute their sheep over the Killin branch and the Callander to Oban, the equivalent of going around three sides of a square. After much sweet talking on Robertson's part the farmers consented to give the new route a trial run and it turned out to be a lot more trouble than it was worth. For a start the Killin railway was surprisingly ill-equipped to handle sheep. For a railway station which ran through predominantly sheep grazing country none of the stations possessed pens or fenced livestock areas and farmers were forced to wait for trains, on the open passenger platforms, amid their sheep. This cannot have been too popular with passengers. With the idea that he had brought the C & O a great amount of business by redirecting farmers over their rails Robertson wrote to them asking that they supply money for improved facilities at Killin and Killin Junction Stations. Nothing came of this request and local farmers soon decided that in future they would travel by Aberfeldy.

~ 13 ~

INTERCHANGE ONLY

The sheep farmers were not the only ones a little unhappy about the lack of facilities and the line's general administrative disorder. The lonely community of people who lived at the head of Glenogle were somewhat unsure of the status which their new station actually held. When the branch line was opened, and Glenoglehead Station was closed to passengers, they expected to be able to board the train at Killin Junction Station. The Killin Railway Company also had this belief but the C & O decided that the only business that the Killin branch would receive was by way of their trains. For this reason they designated the junction station as an interchange platform and no roads were ever built to connect the lonely outpost with the surrounding district. Fortunately through time the rule was relaxed and passengers used the station as they wished. However, as the station had been designed solely as an interchange platform, no overbridge had been erected and those wishing to board the train to Oban had no alternative but to cross the busy tracks on foot. In 1908 a petition was drawn up by local residents and presented to the Killin branch directors demanding a footbridge be built at the station. Had they had the money to meet such a need they surely would have but available funds were tight and the company was unable to put up the bridge. So the junction users put their plea to the Callander to Oban railway offices who consented and built a wooden bridge the

following year. The new bridge, which linked both the up and down platforms, also gave access to the station from a path which had been built to the main road, several hundred yards below the junction. Apart from the metal girders on which the main floor was laid, the bridge was entirely built of timber and painted blue-grey. Almost directly below the footbridge a stream ran beneath the station, through a concrete culvert.

With the opening of the station at Killin, one local man, Peter Stewart, decided that leisure and recreation facilities were a must for weary travellers and asked the Killin directors if he could buy a section of ground between the station and nearby cattle auction. Had they sold him the land he had great plans to turn it into a skating rink and tennis lawn but his proposals were seen as unsuitable and his offer was turned down by the company.

Throughout the Killin branch line's life the management of the Callander to Oban company looked upon it as a small part of their massive railway system and for that reason had no second thoughts about renting out the Killin land for their own gain. In 1905, a Crieff wood merchant, by the name of McAinsh, was scouting around the area in search of a rail connection on the branch for his local forestry interests. However, rather than consult the Killin directors he applied to the C & O who were happy to let a 70 foot long section of ground at Killin Station for the construction of a loading bank. On discovering this plan, and the £3 10s annual rent which the C & O were going to pocket, the Killin directors were furious and told Mr McAinsh that he would have to find alternative methods of moving his timber.

This was probably not a particularly wise move on the part of the directors as financial opportunities did not often present themselves before the railway company. Within the first year of the line's opening, as winter struck its cold wet blow, financial problems began to arise. The building at the junction station leaked badly, particularly on stormy nights and the poorly fitting windows and doors let wind and water into the waiting rooms making life for passengers a little uncomfortable. To add to the problems the station buildings had not been varnished when they were built and the wood soon began to decay. At Killin the position was as bad, if not worse. In addition to

rain water making its way into the waiting room, water from the male urinal also leaked into the passenger quarters. This left Robertson with urgent outstanding repairs and no money with which to make them. He pleaded with the C & O, asking them to carry out the repairs at the junction but to no avail. On the C & O's part they continually pressed the Killin Railway to enlarge Killin Station, a task involving massive capital development and as the directors had little money even for repairs, expansion was out of the question. With an optimistic view towards laying a loop and second platform at Killin, as well as augmenting its flagging income, the railway company had given the Western District of the County of Perth permission to deposit the village refuse at the station. Not surprisingly this was not a very popular move with passengers and no end of complaints were received about the scruffy appearance of the station and the general smell.

80126 at Killin Station

~ 14 ~
POOR COMMUNICATIONS

Communications between the Killin company office and the Callander to Oban railway company were poor, even at the best of times. Although an independent concern Robertson took his orders from Anderson of the C & O, particularly where the junction station was concerned. If he didn't, and if the Killin office decided to start dishing out orders, the C & O could quite easily stop services to the junction and the bulk of the Killin branch trade would disappear.

Arrangements over the junction were high on the list of sore points. Since the first rails had been laid down, arguments and differences of opinion had been rife, even six years after the opening the C & O were managing to dig up skeletons. Arriving in the office one morning Robertson was dismayed to find a bill from Anderson for £53 11s, the wages of a C & O pointsman employed at the junction during its construction. Robertson immediately replied saying that they would not, or rather could not, pay the bill and in doing so he enclosed a bill for the advertising rights at Killin Junction. The rights for each branch station were let at £5 per year and Robertson considered that he was entitled to at least half of the junction revenue as they had paid for the station. Anderson replied in the negative saying that they were entitled to nothing as the junction station did not belong to them. Robertson was furious, and somewhat confused. The Killin Railway company had paid for its erection and had

assumed that in doing so it was their property. Robertson had to concede and accept the fact that as the station was built on C & O land it was indeed C & O property.

For Robertson the acts of some of his villagers, who looked upon free access to their railway in a totally different light from the C & O, strained the already tenuous relationship between the two companies. One stormy night Malcolm McLaren, a Killin villager, set off on his horse to Glenoglehead Station to collect the mails from the evening train. On most occasions the gate leading into the station yard was open, but on this occasion it was bolted shut. Rather than risk leaving his horse unattended outside the station, in case the sudden arrival of a train frightened it, he took the gate off its hinges and led the horse and cart into the yard. Anderson was furious when he learned of the damage to C & O property and threatened McLaren with dire penalties. However Robertson stepped in to save McLaren from wrath of the C & O and the matter was dropped.

Even the natural elements seemed to be against the railway company. During the first year of operation the first blocks of ice that had formed on the River Lochay in some years appeared. The large frozen blocks threatened to damage the narrow wooden piers of the Lochay bridge and so the village blacksmith was called in to fit iron plates to the larch legs. In time, however, the complete structure was replaced with a three span iron girder deck supported on concrete pillars.

For decades the people of Killin had woken in the morning to the peaceful sounds of the surrounding countryside. The famous Falls of Dochart had pounded away on their doorsteps, the wind had whistled through the trees and the birds had twittered on the air. However, with the coming of the railway all this was now to be rudely interrupted by a new noise, the sound of the small engine busily going about its business on the little railway's metals.

Down at Loch Tay the shepherds, out at the crack of dawn, would often look down from the hillside to see the smoke rise from amongst the trees. However, rather than alert the local people of a fire they would know it was just the little loco steaming up before a busy day. People in the village would look out of their windows to see the train pass by before struggling up the steep gradient to the junction. They would see the little engine pull into Killin Station pouring its load of passengers out on to the lonely platforms before reloading with some more and puffing back off up the line. Even at night the beat of an Oban bogie struggling up Glenogle, some five miles away, could be heard echoing through the dark. Then would come the growling rumble of the wee train as it wound its way cautiously down the branch before bursting from the night into Killin Station.

Once the line had opened the Caledonian Railway were happy to operate services over its gleaming metals. For this purpose they supplied two specially built steam engines and the necessary passenger and goods rolling stock. The first public passenger service was run on April 1, 1886 and a generous timetable was supplied. On the same day, the original Killin Station at the head of Glenogle was closed and renamed Glenoglehead Crossing. Although the station ceased to be open to passengers, travellers could notify the guard

at either Lochearnhead or Killin Junction if they wished to alight there. Until 1916, passengers travelling on the Sunday morning down train could often get off or on at Glenoglehead when the early train stopped to set down mail. From then on the station functioned only as a private halt for use by railway staff and as a crossing point.

The first passenger services on the branch were hauled by a specially built 'Killin Pug' locomotive which, in the summer months hauled a rake of some six wooden stagecoach type carriages. Two of the special tank engines were supplied for the line's use. One was stabled permanently on the railway and the other was kept on shed at Stirling and drafted in when required. As the line had limited signalling and no tablet apparatus, in the early days, only one engine could run at any one time. In the summer, however, demand was often so great that the two engines would couple up and haul as many coaches as possible. At one point, between them, they hauled a total of 21 carriages down from the junction to Loch Tay! By contrast the winter months saw no more than a handful of passengers and the railway could operate a skeleton service using only a single locomotive and a composite coach which would run back and forth several times a day, often empty.

Within a short space of time the little railway, with its wee engine, coaches and quaint little stations had become an everyday part of village life. The local villagers were fiercely proud of their new and independent railway.

Before the branch was opened, the Caledonian Railway Company, had agreed to supply stock and operate the concern. The original working agreement between the two companies was that the Caledonian would receive 55% of the gross revenue with a guaranteed minimum of £2,377 over a period of three years.

~ 15 ~

KILLIN PUG

In 1885 top Caley locomotive designer and engineer, Dugald Drummond, was commissioned to build a special small tank engine which could be used on the Killin branch. After much research into the line, its gradients, curves and so on he decided upon an 0-4-2 saddle tank type locomotive. The design was based on the popular 0-4-0 "Pug" tanks which were widely used for dockside and colliery work. Once the plans were prepared two such locomotives were built at the Caledonian Railway's St Rollox locomotive works in Glasgow before being sent up to the branch. Drummond's variations included a pair of trailing wheels which had a diameter of 3 feet. This had allowed him to stretch the locomotive out allowing space for it to carry 800 gallons of water and two and a quarter tons of coal. This meant, unlike many

Immaculate Killin Pug

other saddle tanks, that the Killin pugs would not have to operate trailing a four wheel tender-type coal wagon behind the engine which could have caused problems on the line's short station platforms. They also had parallel shank buffers with large heads and a stovepipe chimney. The two engines were originally painted in a gleaming Caledonian blue livery with maroon underframes and black and white lining. The number plates were of polished brass with black wax-filled letters and figures.

With its tall, straight stovepipe chimney the little engine soon became known as the coffee pot amongst the local villagers who would often gather on the station platforms when the train was due just to marvel at its sheer size and power. It may have only been a small engine by comparison to the larger mainline giants, but to the people of Killin nothing could have beaten their blue pug. From the first thoughts of a railway right through to its completion and long years of operation, the line had been very much a part of the tightly knitted Highland community which existed in Killin like that of many other small Scottish towns and villages. It had been funded solely by the villagers and their laird and as a result had become very dear to their hearts. There was a proud feeling of independence about the railway which was to last right into the days of the Big Four grouping and up until then the locals fought hard to retain that quality.

The long list of shareholders shows just what a community effort the project was. It included many ordinary men and women who parted with hard earned money in order to help finance the railway which was to benefit them all in some way or other despite the fact that the shares rarely paid any dividends. Many were just local merchants and shop keepers such as the village grocer who bought a single share and the local parish minister who invested in two. Other traders with an interest in the line included the village dressmaker, the shoemaker, the draper, the saddler and a local gardener all of whom had one or two shares. The shareholders list also shows which trades were the most lucrative in the area at the time.

The area's wool-merchant had a total of eight shares to his name.

The top ten shareholders read as follows:

Earl of Breadalbane	2015	shares.
Callander & Oban Rly. Co.	1200	
Sir Donald Currie	200	
Charles Stewart	200	
John Willison	200	
John Cameron	200	
Hon Ivan Campbell	60	
R.A. Robertson	12	
B .& J. Campbell	10	
D.I. McDiarmid	10	

Of these shareholders the first Board of Directors was elected as follows:

Chairman	Earl of Breadalbane, Taymouth Castle.
Dpt Chairman	Charles Stewart, Tighndruim, Killin.
	Sir Donald Currie, Garth, Aberfeldy.
	John Willison, Killin.
	John Cameron, Killin.

The first train crew, who drove the train on the railway's ceremonial opening day, were all local men, and at points in the line's history, women were also employed. In addition to the first train crew, Watt and his fireman Dick, there was also a full complement of surfacemen, passenger guards and station porters. Houses were supplied in the village for the guard and station staff and a cottage was built under the Dochart Viaduct for the railway's surfaceman who tended to the five miles of track. Cottages were later provided for the footplatemen at Loch Tay pier, at a rental of 1s 9d per week. However both Watt and Dick were far from perfect tenants and paid not a single penny in rent. This was perhaps the reason for their sudden disappearance from the company's books in 1889 when they were replaced by Messrs Summer and Winterbottom. The surfaceman who rented the cottage by the viaduct, at 15s per year, also found himself two years behind with the rent so, when confronted with the problem bank manager Robertson was forced to deduct the sum from future wages.

The wee train had been functioning for only a few months when the first problems began to arise over the contract drawn up with the Caledonian Railway Company. The Caley had been paying the Killin office a portion of the traffic receipts each month as agreed but very soon it became clear that operational revenue was never likely to reach the £2,377 guaranteed by the Killin directors so the Caledonian decided that they had every right to retain all revenue from the line and not a single penny made its way into the Killin company funds. This left the wee line with more than a few problems. With no money coming in they were unable to pay for any work or other expenses and, with Christmas near, interest on the company bonds was due. The only way that Robertson could pay this and other expenses was to take money from the capital account - a dubious if not downright illegal exercise.

In a bid to resolve the matter Robertson tried hard to organise an urgent meeting between the Caledonian men and the Killin directors. After weeks of letter writing Robertson eventually managed to arrange a meeting in Glasgow and even asked for free travel passes to be sent to the Killin directors. With little forward planning Robertson was eventually on his way to Glasgow, formulating his case against the CR on board one of their own trains. The main point of Robertson's trip was to squeeze some money from the Caledonian and before leaving his Highland enclave, Robertson is reported to have said, "We must just try and get as much out of them as possible."

Robertson's trip, however, did prove to be a success and a new working agreement was reached whereby the Caledonian would work the line at cost for a period of five years and contribute £525 to the Killin office to pay the secretary's salary and interest on loans. The new contract would be renewed at five yearly intervals.

Following the line's first ten months of operation Robertson was bound by the Board of Trade Regulation of Railways Act to submit an operational report to the Board. In it he stated that the company had operated at least six trains a day in the summer and winter months without even the slightest accident. During the summer services were run by the loco and normally two passenger carriages and in the winter the company struggled by, using their composite coach. The results of the first ten months of operation, from April 1, 1886 to January 21, 1887 looked promising and a profit was shown on the company books.

Revenue for 10 months

	£	s	d
Passenger	517	6	9
Parcels, horses, carriages	102	7	0
Goods	444	19	8
Minerals	206	16	1
Live stock	46	9	5
Mails	33	4	6
	1351	3	5

General charges for 10 months.

	£	s	d
Secretary's salary	50	0	0
Auditor's fee	10	10	0
Fee for registration		13	6
Fee for assessor		5	0
Fire insurance	3	8	10
Auditor's travelling expenses		12	0
Repairs		17	9
Postage and telegrams	2	7	1
	68	14	2
Government duty	5	2	1

Rates and Taxes.

	£	s	d
Poor & school as proprietor	9	5	10
Poor & school as occupier	9	15	10
Road tax as proprietor	5	9	6
Road tax as occupier	4	3	1

By 1889 the Caledonian Railway Company were beginning to experience difficulties with the specially designed Killin Pug locomotives and both were withdrawn and relocated to shed duties in Aberdeen. In their place the train crews had larger and more powerful 0-4-4 Caledonian tank locomotives to contend with. Built at the St Rollox works sometime between 1884 and 1889 the two engines, again designed by Dugald Drummond, were suited to rural passenger work and had already proved popular elsewhere in Scotland. CR No. 1177 and 1175 were both allocated to the branch with 1177 being stabled in the shed at Loch Tay and 1175 kept on shed in Stirling. With their large twin front driving wheels and excellent tractive effort they were perfect for the branch's steep gradient and continued on the line well into the 1950s.

LMS No 15103 at Loch Tay shed

LMS No 15103 on Killin Branch train, 28.7.31

~ 16 ~

TOURISTS GALORE

From the outset tourism was to play a major role in the little railway's livelihood. In the summer months traffic was always at its best, sometimes there were so many people wishing to travel on the line that the staff and the wee train could just not cope. Often, even with a direct telephone line, communications became muddled between Killin Junction and Killin stations and the station staff in the village didn't quite know what to expect on a busy summer afternoon. On one occasion great embarrassment was caused to the railway company and staff when three locomotives, tripleheading a combined total of 21 coaches, full of holiday tourists, arrived at Killin Station's short railway platforms. Being long enough only to accommodate three coaches at any one time the train had to unload in no less than seven stages!

Through time and experience the railway company soon became able to cope with the busy traffic of the early years which escalated beyond their wildest dreams. Tourists, travellers and assorted visitors came from all over Britain to sample the unique Highland flavour of Killin and nearby Loch Tay. The village was then as much of a tourist trap as it is now with people travelling from miles around to view the surrounding hills, take to the waters of the loch or sit by the famous Falls of Dochart which still thunder dramatically through the centre of the sleepy village. The affluent Victorian people of the day liked nothing more

than to sample life, and fresh air, away from their homes and factories in the big smog-choked cities. To cater for the ever increasing demand, hotels, shops and inns grew up in the village to serve the long distance travellers who would arrive daily by rail.

One of the busiest holiday periods was the start of the shooting season when wealthy families from the south arrived to take accommodation in the area's many shooting lodges. Invariably they would arrive with every possible artefact that they would need over the summer, including their own horses, dogs, furniture, carts and much more besides. All of these items, plus passengers, would arrive at Killin Junction by train and have to be fitted on to the wee train. Such days would play havoc with any preset timetable once time had been made to hitch up any extra horse vans or if too much luggage existed for a single journey, several trips would be made.

The wealthy visitors also brought with them their gillies who were not adverse to the odd practical joke, often at the expense of the local villagers as one Killin farmer found to his cost. He had travelled down by car to Killin Station to collect a friend from the last day's train and, as it was delayed, he left his car in the yard and went into the station to have a chat with the stationmaster. Outside a crowd of gillies had just emerged from the local hotel and were staggering through the station car park. When the train finally arrived the farmer and his friend left the station and headed for the car which they attempted to drive off until a loud clattering noise and a voice shouting 'Stop thief' halted them in their tracks. After investigating the farmer found to his dismay that the drunken gillies had tied the two wheeled station barrow to his rear bumper!

However one of the most notable collection of eccentrics to be involved with the railway were the men who drove the wee train in its final years of service. All were well known in the village and all had nick-names by which they were known. Douglas Campbell, a porter at Killin Station was known as the 'bear', Bob Black, who operated the yard crane at Killin was the 'billy goat' and the local favourite, a rogue named Martin Lawrie, was called the 'boar'. Martin was probably the most cheeky of the happy, friendly and helpful station staff, although this did not stop him having the odd quarrel with his neighbours, especially the parish minister. Martin, a train guard on the line, lived in one of the railway company cottages which, of course, were not fitted with such modern facilities as running water. Instead, he obtained his from a tap sited outside his front door. However on one cold and frosty winter's morning Martin went out into the cold to fill his kettle but as he twisted the tap on, the top shot off leaving a shower of water spurting from the pipe. At that point the local minister, Reverend Thomson, passed by the cottage.

"What would you do with that, Mr Thomson?" Martin called to the passing clergyman.

"It obviously calls for a plumber," came the reply from the reverend.

Being proud of his job on the railway Martin requested that the minister call in the plumber as he had to go to work, and at any rate the minister only worked one day a week!

"As far as you are concerned, I haven't got a day at all," said the minister as he stomped off.

However the tale had a happy ending. The tap was fixed and Martin was in church that Sunday. It did, however, demonstrate just how highly the railway and its staff were rated in the village community.

One railway employee and his wife were thought to have such strange ideas that they were christened Mr and Mrs Harpic, clean round the bend, by the other villagers. Obviously the giant world of advertising had not passed the quiet and isolated Highland glen by!

The little railway even attracted the attention of Queen Victoria who visited the area at the turn of the century and was so impressed by the dark and forbidding Glenogle, that she named it the Kyber Pass of the Highlands. Just prior to the closure of the Callander to Crianlarich line in 1965, the present Queen Elizabeth had been expected to travel up Glenogle to open the then new hydro-electric power station at Falls of Cruachan but a rockfall in the pass forced the royal party to chose another route north.

~ 17 ~

THE LOCH TAY STEAMERS

One of the area's greatest honey pots was Loch Tay. The fresh clear waters stretched out between the gently rolling valley sides which separated the loch from the high mountains which flanked it on all fronts. During the summer folk flocked from all corners of Britain to Killin, many just to experience the magic of the loch and its surrounding countryside. The Marquis of Breadalbane had not overlooked the potential which the inshore loch held and in 1882, prior to the opening of the railway, he put a passenger steam ship into service on the calm waters. The first vessel, named *The Lady of the Lake* (which was something of an odd title for a Scottish vessel) was a 92-foot long craft built from oak especially for the newly formed Loch Tay Steamboat Company which, like the railway, was another of Breadalbane's business ventures. *The Lady*, as she became known locally, had the capacity to hold 100 passengers and operated the first regular passenger service from Kenmore down the loch to Killin. At that

Killin Pier

Six Lochs Tour at Killin Station

point no roads existed on the lochside and the only way to move about was on drovers' tracks and sheep paths. With the opening of the branch line, the Loch Tay steamers, which were originally laid on for the benefit of local people, experienced a massive boost in popularity with tourists and visitors taking to the water. With the completion of Loch Tay Station a wooden pier, with a set of rails, was projected out into the loch to meet the boats.

Cruises proved to be most popular on the long summer evenings. Passengers would travel along from Killin on the branch line extension before boarding *The Lady* which sailed round the loch, calling at Kenmore on the north-eastern tip of the loch, before returning to Killin. At the turn of the century the demand for cruises became so great that the Loch Tay Steamboat Company commissioned the Ailsa Shipbuilding Company of Troon to supply them with a second, larger vessel. On March 19, 1907 the new addition to the fleet,

christened *The Queen of the Lake*, arrived at Killin. Never one to let trade pass him by, the Marquis insisted that the wooden sections be transported north on the Callander and Oban line before being transferred to his branch line. From Loch Tay pier the vessel parts were loaded on to a freight barge and taken up to Kenmore where the ship was assembled and launched. Weighing 152 tons and measuring 110 feet in length, *The Queen* soon became popular with both individuals and charter parties.

A whole host of special tours and cheap day tickets were soon organised to make use of both the local rail network and the Loch Tay steamers. One of the first was a round tour leaving Glasgow and Edinburgh early in the morning, taking the travellers up Glenogle then on to the Killin branch where they were displaced on to one of the cruise ships. After taking lunch aboard the ship, the relaxed passengers would sail up Loch Tay to Kenmore at a leisurely pace before heading to Aberfeldy by road on a motor coach. Once there the tour would return south on the Aberfeldy branch and the Highland Railway via Perth. An earlier Caledonian Railway package, aptly named 'Railway Trip and the Sail', was certainly not going to supply traffic to their Caley's competitors and involved a rail journey up to Killin and a round trip on Loch Tay. Such a day tour cost 7/6d from Edinburgh and 7/-d from Glasgow which included a third class cabin on the boat. The complete trip, including a ten minute stop in Kenmore, took about 10 hours from Edinburgh with almost half of this spent on the water. During the British Railways era, the famous Six Lochs tour was run via Loch Tay and the Killin branch. Green three-car multiple units operated the trip which called at Loch Lubnaig, the west tip of Loch Earn, Loch Tay, where the travellers had lunch before travelling home via Crianlarich and Loch Lomond, Loch Long and Gare Loch.

In addition to the more glamorous passenger services which regularly plied the loch, the Loch Tay Steamboat Company also operated two cargo vessels for the benefit of local farmers and merchants. The first, named *Carlotta*, was introduced in 1883 to meet the demands of local traders and shepherds. She was regularly used by lochside inhabitants as a means of taking their produce, in the form of cattle, sheep, vegetables or wool to the markets in Killin at the west end of the loch and Aberfeldy in the east. In this way the Marquis could encourage farmers to use the railway by guiding them to Killin. *Carlotta* was no stranger to the wide range of cargoes which were forced upon her. These often included livestock, timber, coal and even minerals, such as copper ore which the Marquis extracted from a mining interest on the south shore of the loch. Several years later a second cargo boat was built to the same design and named *Sybilla*.

BR Green DMU on Six Lochs Tour crossing Dochart Viaduct

~ 18 ~

TROUBLED WATERS

The "wee train" continued to wind its way up and down the village railway until it finally puffed into the 20th century, a time when it would see the most drastic changes in its short history. In summer visitors continued to come in droves, either to stay in Killin village or to sample the delights of the Loch Tay Steamers. However, in winter few people travelled on the railway and the single-coach train, which happily plied the sleepy little line, saw only a handful of passengers. There were times on the quiet little railway when even the company secretary was out of touch with the daily goings-ons on the country line. On October 24, 1917 fire tore through the Loch Tay pier engine shed destroying the building. In Killin the dramatic event was the talking point amongst locals for some days, but Mr E. MacEwan, who had succeeded Robertson as company secretary, knew nothing of the incident until almost a week later when he received a letter from the Callander and Oban Railway Company asking if he had claimed the insurance money. Apparently whoever had reported the fire had gone to the C & O offices rather than those of the Killin Railway Company.

"I regret to report that the engine shed at Loch Tay Pier Station was totally destroyed by fire on the morning..." he reported to Breadalbane. At the same time MacEwan contacted the railway company's insurance brokers only to find that their shed had been under-insured. However the company paid out the full policy for £120 and this was passed on to the Caledonian who, MacEwan hoped, would make up the difference for a new shed. Some days later the cheque was cashed in by the Caledonian and MacEwan took this as a sign that a replacement structure would be forthcoming.

The winter and spring of 1922/23 saw events which signalled the start of the Killin railway's slow decline, which was to continue until its eventual closure some forty years later. The line's founder, the Marquis of Breadalbane, died on October 19, 1922 and with this the railway's future became very uncertain.

Gavin Campbell, the Third Marquis of Breadalbane, whose estate covered some 400,000 acres of land extending right across central Scotland, played a great role in driving railway's into the Highlands. For many years he was a director of the Caledonian Railway Company and gave facilities for the passing of the West Highland Railway through his property from Ardlui to Achallader. For over a year prior to his death, the Marquis had been

No. 55173 Class 0-4-4 at Killin Station, 1961.

in poor health but insisted on attending to his numerous duties. It was while in Glasgow, at a meeting of railway directors, that he suddenly took ill and died in the city's Central Hotel at the age of 71.

His trustees were not disposed to regard the village line in the same paternal light as the late chairman and ceased funding the cause any further. With this MacEwan and the two remaining directors, John Cameron and John Willison, did what they could to keep the concern functioning. To add to the already hefty problems, the Killin Railway Company had amassed debts of over £12,000 and had not paid a single share dividend for almost twenty years. At the same time Britain's railway network was on the brink of undergoing the greatest upheaval in its entire history, the Big Four Grouping of 1923, and unfortunately the three men had only a hazy idea of what the railway political scene of 1922/23 held in store for them.

Firstly they thought that the Caledonian Railway Company was the absorbing power but then correspondence began arriving from London and they were under the impression that they were soon to become part of the London and North Western Railway Company. Eventually terms for a take-over of the line and its debts were received from the giant London Midland and Scottish Railway Company. The Killin directors met to consider the offer, not fully sure of who their predators were, and replied in the negative. The LMS were surprised, they had offered to accept all the company's debts, and in addition pay £1 in cash for every £100 of Killin stock. However the Killin directors thought the offer insulting, and resolved to demand £10 for every £100 of stock. Dealing with the Killin directors was Arthur Watson who duly passed that matter over to Donald Matheson, an ex-Caledonian man who had taken up the position of Scottish deputy manager with the LMS. Shortly after receiving the following short note from the indignant directors of the Killin railway, he replied to say that better terms would be forthcoming.

```
                                   Killin Rly Office,
                                   17 January 1923,

Dear Sir,
Your letter of 8 inst was duly submitted to
my directors who have instructed me to reply
that they regret they cannot accept the
terms offered.
     Yours faithfully,
     E. MacEwan, Sec.

Arthur Watson, Esq.,
LMSR, General Manager's Office,
Euston, London.
```

For a company with such impressive debts, no rolling stock of their own and few assets, the letter seemed to be biting the hand that was prepared to feed them, but it did the trick for the directors. Advertising the line as a going concern, a second letter from the Killin secretary was sent to the LMS in a bid to explain why the railway had shown such poor results and it further offered reasons why the Killin branch was worth more that £1 per £100. Matheson admitted that the disastrous coal strike of 1921 had put restrictions on the line, but he saw financial salvation in the recently revived timber traffic. MacEwan continued by trying to persuade the LMS that the Killin branch was a valuable link in the system they operated. With the branch the Callander and Oban line could be connected up with the ex-Highland Railway at the east end of Loch Tay via the steam boats and a motorbus service.

Before a second offer was made, the LMS instructed the Killin company to prepare an inventory of station fittings and a personal questionnaire revealed that 63-year-old MacEwan earned just £30 per annum from the Killin Railway Company. When asked to complete a list of office fittings he revealed that every item belonged to either himself or the Bank of Scotland from whom the Killin railway had received free quarters during its 40 years

in business. On March 9, 1923 John Cameron and MacEwan met LMS representatives in Glasgow and were offered £7 10s in cash of each £100 worth of stock. Again they rejected the offer and decided to fight for their independence. A letter was sent to the LMS asking for £10 per £100 and, by return, they received an offer of £8 per £100. MacEwan arranged a meeting of the dozen remaining shareholders and the chairman announced that after consulting experienced lawyers and accountants and after fully considering all the facts the board was of the opinion - although the final decision was a matter for the shareholders - that the LMS offer should be accepted. The shareholders approved the motion although they expressed the hope that free passes would be issued to the Killin directors, and the secretary, who had charged nothing for their services over the final years of independence. The meeting was closed and the final entry was made in the Killin board minute book: "A hearty vote of thanks accorded to the chairman brought the meeting to a close."

To the end the secretary sought to impress everybody with the importance of the railway. In sending hand-written copies of the accounts to the LMS he apologised with the remark, "I am without a typist," implying that perhaps the typist was ill. However the Killin office had never owned anything as modern, or expensive, as a typewriter, let alone a typist. On June 1, 1923, MacEwan took the step of instructing the village joiner to make a strong case in which to despatch the seal and books to London and the railway lost its last threads of independence which had once made it so popular with the local villagers.

Once in the hands of the LMS, the railway was slowly run down. In 1939 the Loch Tay steamers were withdrawn and broken up at Kenmore and the pier at Loch Tay Station was destroyed. At the same time Loch Tay Station was closed to passengers although the track remained in-situ to the engine shed.

~ 19 ~

BRITISH RAILWAYS

On the first day of 1948, the Killin branch fell into the hands of British Railways with the nationalisation of the entire British railway network. For the folk in Killin the largest shake-up in railway history meant little more than an eventual change in engine number and rolling stock livery. In the decade between 1952 and 1962, an assortment of motive power worked the branch until the giant BR Standard 2-6-4

4MT engines took over until closure. Based on an original LMS design, the massive engines, which were especially suited to mixed traffic, dwarfed the small stations on the Killin branch and even made the mighty Dochart Viaduct pale into insignificance.

Designed by Mr R.A. Riddles and built in Brighton, the engines were introduced in July 1951 and used widely on the original LMS

80093 and Southbound train at Killin Junction.

routes with many being stabled in Glasgow. The mainstay of operations on the Killin branch was 80126 which was stabled there from 1962 until closure. The second engine allocated to the line, but kept on shed in Stirling, was 80092 with 80093 and 80028 making regular appearances at Killin over the years.

The last major peak in operations occurred in 1950 when the Hydro-Electric Board used the line from Killin Junction to Loch Tay during the construction of a new hydro-electric power station sited just yards from the terminus. Taking water from a newly-built dam on Lochan na Lairige, the generating station supplied power to the houses in Killin and took several years to complete, in which time the Killin railway enjoyed a much needed boost in revenue.

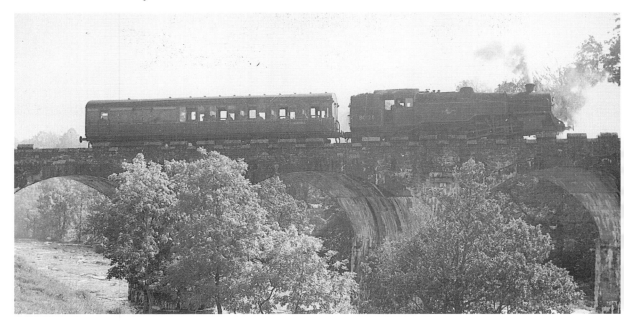

BR 2-6-4 80126 on Dochart Viaduct

BR 2-6-4 loco with branch train between Killin and Killin Junction

~ 20 ~

CLOSURE

Villagers, well wrapped up against the chill autumn rain, turned out to wave a final goodbye to the wee train as it pulled out of Killin Station for the last time on September 27, 1965. Although the planned closure, under Dr Beeching's famous railway act, was set for November of that year, a rockfall in Glenogle had stopped all mainline traffic and the opportunity was taken to close the branch. In fact many locals believed that the fatal landslide may have been started deliberately in order to allow British Railways to close the Callander to Crianlarich line and its branches whilst at the same time having enough ammunition to fight the tide of public opposition which was likely to rise from the decision.

When a party of railway engineers visited the glen prior to closure, it was announced that repairs would cost in excess of £30,000 before the railway could be re-opened to traffic. However one local minister claimed that the debris could be cleared for only £100. A bitter feud followed between BR and the Highland population until the minister was visited one night by the engineer who had made the estimate. Accusing the clergyman of casting doubt on his professional judgement, the engineer invited the minister on to the track to view the damage for himself. The following morning, after a long trek up the glen in the pouring rain, they reached the spot where a fall of boulders blocked the path. The minister pointed out the small pile of rock on the line

and upheld his £100 view at which the engineer thrust him a spade and said, "clear it and I'll give you £100!"

Suffice to say, the line stayed blocked and the decision to close the railway as far as Crianlarich was upheld. On the fateful day of the rockfall, September 26, some special trains which had been run in connection with the Glasgow holiday had to be diverted back to the city via the North British route from Crianlarich, and the last traffic on the Killin branch the next day acted purely as a mopping up operation.

On that wet and grim day at Killin Station most of the locals had braved the elements to see the train, which many had known and loved over the years, pull out of the station for the breakers yard in Glasgow. As fog signals, placed along the track, cracked a last sad salute to the train, it seemed that the send-off celebrations were somewhat premature. Folk cheered as it became obvious that even the train did not want to go. As the locomotive, BR Standard 4MT 2-6-4T No. 80093, with its load of three coaches and 13 wagons set off from the station, the complete train stopped 200 yards or so from the platform. It turned out that the drizzle had made the rails so greasy that the loco wheels could not grip and the steam engine was forced to return to the station with its heavy load. Running back some distance, the train took a longer run at the 1 in 50 gradient but a cloud of smoke above the trees a quarter of a mile from the village showed that it had become stuck again! Back through the station the train crawled and another attempt was made, this time without the 13 wagons. Third time lucky and the train finally made its somewhat reluctant departure. At Killin Junction, 80093, which had been the branch's mainstay of operations throughout its final years, left its carriages to return to Killin for the wagons before setting off, bound for Crianlarich with its full load, over half an hour late. From there driver John Milne, fireman Alexander Hunter and guard Martin Lawrie, took a taxi back to Killin while another crew drove the train on the final lap of the journey, to Glasgow.

Up in the hills above Killin at Acharn Farm, 84-year-old Mr Douglas Willison - the only living villager who saw the first train pull into Killin Station in 1887 - was at the sheep dipping as the engine steamed along above the pens to Killin Junction.

Prior to the early closure, the residents of Killin had fought hard in a desperate bid to retain their railway service. A rail closure protest committee was formed and a petition carrying some 500 names was sent by the chairman, Rev. John Colquhoun of Killin and Ardeonaig Parish Church, to the Secretary of State for Transport who had passed it on to Mr Tom Fraser, Minister of Transport. However, despite this, closure went ahead.

With nothing to meet the Killin train any longer at the lonely Killin Junction exchange platform, a bus service through the village, including a school service which left Crianlarich at 7.25am and travelled to Callander via Killin, began on September 28 and the railway was all but gone.

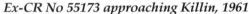

Ex-CR No 55173 approaching Killin, 1961

~ 21 ~

Final Years

In its final years the railway employed a staff of seven at Killin including a stationmaster, two drivers, two firemen and two guards, all of whom faced transfer or redundancy. However as many were local men whose families had lived in Killin for centuries, redundancy proved to be the most popular option. In the last years of operation, the timetable changed very little and the railway relied on services to and from Killin Junction for its income. Daily runs were also made from Killin to Callander with over 150 local schoolchildren using the train to go to and from school. The summer continued to bring its share of visitors who could now travel only as far as Killin. Between Killin and Loch Tay, ashes were spread on the track which was used as a walkway. This practise was quite safe as the section of line was only used to ferry the engine back and forth between Killin Station and its shed.

British Railways Class 4MT 2-6-4T No. 80093, smartly turned out in black livery had provided the motive power for the branch's last three years of operation with assistance supplied by sister locos 80126 and 80023 among others. A solitary LNER four compartment brake carriage kept the giant engine company as the pair plied up and down between Killin and Killin Junction being more than adequate for the quiet and little used autumn services. However no matter how insignificant the train, the departures from Killin were still as noisy and as exuberant as the day the first train ran and the downhill run from the Junction was carried out with the same panache. Fewer than 50 passengers would be carried on the line in any one day and many of these on a highly unofficial basis.

At Killin the station had fallen into a forgotten state of repair. For visitors, finding the unsigned station was difficult enough in itself. Despite plans to build a loop at the station, nothing ever became of the second set of rails and the station ended its years with a single platform. Weather worn and warped with age, the main station building, from which sprouted the familiar enamel sign 'You may telephone from here', stood proud on the edge of the village. With no booking office, passengers had merely to tap on a window, which opened directly on to the platform, to be issued with tickets for Crianlarich, Luib, Balquhidder or wherever your destination lay. Anywhere, that is, except Killin Junction which, until its end, acted only as an exchange platform. As no loop had ever been built at the station, gravity shunting was the order of the day. The vigorous fly-shunting was necessary to get the engine back to the head of the train and involved unhitching the carriages before driving the engine into the goods siding. With a hefty shove and much gaelic swearing the coaches were pushed a short way up the line to allow the loco to scuttle into the siding. The free-wheeling coaches would then run down

Killin in its final years.

the slight incline unaided and come to a halt on the Lochay bridge. The engine thereupon rejoined her charge, and dragged it back alongside the single platform. Once complete, there was usually plenty of time for a lengthy chat with the stationmaster before the arrival of the passengers for Killin Junction and beyond.

At Killin Junction the station remained unchanged up until its final day of closure. Latterly hemmed in by Forestry Commission pine trees, the slender lattice-work signal posts proudly carried their Caledonian Railway semaphore arms up until the end. Decorative oil lamps hung from simple wooden posts, at night, casting a wavering ray of light on the antique signs and station nameboards. Wear and tear over the years had left many of the stone-edged platforms bearing huge baulks of timber, instead of the customary stone or brick. Right down to the sagging roofs, warped woodwork and flaking paint, the junction

station had fallen into the same sorry state of repair as the old station at Killin.

Ironically the only station to boast an almost pristine condition was Loch Tay which had been the first to close in 1939. Bought privately and converted into a house, the building exists to this day as a holiday residence. By 1965 the Loch Tay section of the branch survived primarily to allow the branch engine access to its shed, a sub-shed of Stirling, which had almost become lost in the dense vegetation which was slowly engulfing the railway. By the shed a water column fed the engine with its liquid and a makeshift coaling stage had been erected on the Loch Tay Station loop utilising several redundant old metal mineral wagons.

Despite losing its independence with the grouping, the little railway still retained something of its original character and charm which made it a firm favourite with the villagers right up to the end. After being closed to passenger traffic in 1939, few local people took any notice of the restrictions placed on the Loch Tay section of line and many would ride happily down to the shed in the loco cab with the driver. Trips from Killin to Loch Tay, to see the engine being watered and coaled, also proved popular with the local children and the drivers were only too happy to load a dozen or so youngsters up on the footplate for the ride.

In its entire history the Killin railway never once surrendered its metals to the wheels of a diesel locomotive. Despite the fact they passed through Killin Junction daily never once did they stray on to the branch. However with the sudden closure all these scenes became just a memory, held in the mind, and on film, by all those who had travelled on the railway at some point in its 80 year history.

Shortly after the line's closure the tracks were lifted along with those of the C & O and the station buildings were slowly allowed to fall into disrepair. At the junction the main station building, platforms and footbridge were destroyed to make way for tree-planting leaving just part of the island platform dwarfed by pines. The station houses remain, derelict and have since been bought for renovation. The signal box was emptied on closure and

bulldozed leaving a pile of red bricks, timber and cracked drainpipes which remain scattered around the site to this day. The trackbed down to Killin remains open to allow access to the forestry plantations, although the bridge over the A85 at Lix Toll has since disappeared to make way for road development. Other bridges and culverts still exist and the odd telephone pole, minus its wires, still stands as a tribute to the railway.

The Acharn siding was lifted with the branch although a gate and part of the two-lever ground-frame exist in the undergrowth. Flanking the disused trackbed are occasional piles of concrete sleepers which were left with no purpose to serve after the track was lifted and removed. Nearer Killin the trackbed has made way for house-building and development and the site where Killin Station once stood is now used as a scrapyard. Where the goods trains once unloaded their cargoes is now a car park and road depot operated by Central Regional Council. Both the Dochart Viaduct and the metal girder bridge spanning the River Lochay still stand, used by walkers now having not seen the wheels of a train for over 20 years.

TICKETS

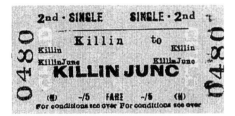

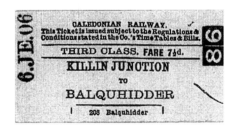

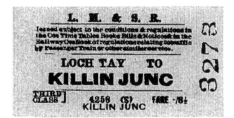

CHRONOLOGY OF EVENTS

1	June	1870	Callander to Killin section of the C & O railway opened.
	August	1873	Killin to Tyndrum section opened.
		1881	The Third Marquis of Breadalbane approaches C & O Rly Co to build branch to Killin.
19	Oct.	1882	First meeting of Killin Railway Company in the Drill Hall, Killin.
		1882	*Lady of the Lake* steamship introduced to Loch Tay.
	July	1883	Work begins on the Killin branch.
		1883	Cargo steamer *Carlotta* introduced on to Loch Tay.
	Nov.	1884	Contractor's funds arrested.
13	March	1886	Ceremonial opening of branch line.
1	April	1886	Killin Branch Railway opened to passengers.
			Killin renamed Glenoglehead on opening.
		1889	Killin Pugs withdrawn from branch.
19	July	1907	*Queen of the Lake* launched on Loch Tay.
		1908	Footbridge erected at Killin Junction.
4	Oct.	1917	Branch engine shed destroyed by fire.
19	Oct.	1922	The Third Marquis of Breadalbane died.
19	March	1923	Branch absorbed by LMS. Last meeting of Killin Railway Company shareholders.
		1923	Cargo steamer *Carlotta* withdrawn from Loch Tay.
		1929	Cargo steamer *Sybilla* withdrawn from Loch Tay.
9	Sept.	1939	Killin to Loch Tay section of branch closed to traffic. Pier at Loch Tay destroyed and steamers withdrawn and broken up.
1	Jan.	1948	Branch absorbed by British Railways.
		1950	Branch used during construction of Hydro-Electric power station near Loch Tay Station.
7	Nov.	1964	Freight withdrawn from branch.
27	Sept.	1965	Killin branch, Crianlarich Lower to Callander closed completely due to landslide. Last train leaves Killin Station.
	Nov.	1965	Dr Beeching's planned closure of the Killin branch.

The above chronology is a brief listing of events and dates affecting the Killin Branch Railway, all of which can be found, in greater detail, throughout the book.

UP

		am	am	am	am	pm	pm	pm	pm
Loch Tay	dep	—	—	8.55	11.35	2.15	—	5.50	—
Killin	arr	—	—	8.59	11.38	2.18	—	5.53	—
Killin	dep	6.45	7.35	9.01	11.40	2.23	4.15	6.00	6.50
Killin Jct	arr	6.58	7.48	9.15	11.53	2.37	4.28	6.13	7.33

DOWN

		am	am	am	pm	pm	pm	pm	pm
Killin Jct	dep	7.12	8.04	10.25	12.30	2.50	4.55	6.30	7.12
Killin	arr	7.25	8.18	10.38	12.44	3.03	5.08	6.45	7.26
Killin	dep	—	8.20	10.40	1.40	—	5.26	—	—
Loch Tay	arr	—	8.24	10.43	1.44	—	5.29	—	—

Note: The 11.35, 2.15 and 4.15 up trains and the 12.30, 2.50 and 7.12 down trains were all mixed goods. Other goods services were run without timetable.

TIMETABLE 2: CALEDONIAN RAILWAY CO. SUMMER TIMETABLE, JULY 1922.

UP

		am	am	am	pm	pm	pm	pm	pm
Loch Tay	dep	—	9.35	—	12.15	1.25	—	—	6.35
Killin	arr	—	9.38	—	12.19	1.29	—	—	6.39
Killin	dep	7.15	9.40	10.30	12.21	1.31	2.35	5.32	7.15
Killin Jct	arr	7.28	9.54	10.43	12.35	1.45	2.48	5.45	7.25

DOWN

		am	am	am	pm	pm	pm	pm	pm
Killin Jct	dep	7.40	10.07	10.55	12.50	2.00	3.05	6.00	7.35
Killin	arr	7.54	10.20	11.08	1.03	2.14	3.18	6.13	8.12
Killin	dep	8.45	—	11.10	1.10	—	—	6.15	—
Loch Tay	arr	8.49	—	11.14	1.14	—	—	6.19	—

TIMETABLE 3: EDINBURGH AND GLASGOW TO LOCH TAY.

Caledonian Railway Co. Steamers ~ Railways Timetable July 1922.

Weekdays only

		am	am	am	am
Edinburgh	dep	—	6.45	9.25	11.30
Oban	"	—	8.45	—	3.50
Glasgow	dep	—	7.40	10.10	12.00
Killin Pier (Steamer)	"	—	11.30	1.30	6.30
Ardeonaig	"	—	12.10	—	6.55
Lawers	"	—	12.35	—	7.10
Ardtalnaig	"	—	12.55	—	7.15
Fearnan	"	—	1.20	—	7.40
Kenmore Pier	"	—	2.02	2.55	8.00
Kenmore Pier (Motor)	dep	11.40	3.00	3.08	8.05
Aberfeldy (Motor)	arr	12.15	3.35	3.35	8.40

		am	am	pm	pm
Aberfeldy (Motor)	dep	—	11.00	1.15	6.00
Kenmore (Motor)	arr	—	11.35	1.50	6.25
Kenmore Pier (Steamer)	dep	7.00	11.40	4.30	—
Fearnan	"	7.25	—	4.50	—
Ardtalnaig	"	7.50	—	5.10	—
Lawers	"	8.00	—	5.15	—
Ardeonaig	"	8.25	—	5.30	—
Killin Pier (Train)	arr	9.10	—	6.15	—
Glasgow	"	1.16	—	10.15	—
Oban	arr	12.07	—	9.50	—
Edinburgh	"	1.52	—	10.20	—

TIMETABLE 4: THE LAST LMS TIMETABLE, 1947.

Killin and Loch Tay

Glasgow	dep	4.20	8.00	—	2.10	5.10
Edinburgh	"	—	6.50	—	11.44	4.23
Oban	"	6.05	—	9.10	12.05	5.15
Killin Jct	dep	8.12	10.30	11.18	2.50	7.36
Killin	arr	8.25	10.42	11.30	3.02	7.48
Killin	dep	—	—	—	—	—
Loch Tay	arr	—	—	—	—	—
Loch Tay	dep	—	—	—	—	—
Killin	arr	—	—	—	—	—
Killin	dep	7.45	10.05	10.55	1.42	6.55
Killin Jct	arr	7.58	10.19	11.08	1.56	7.08
Oban	arr	—	12.27	—	4.38	9.25
Edinburgh	arr	11.00	—	2.25	4.39	10.04
Glasgow	arr	10.15	—	1.34	4.23	9.31

Third Class only between Killin Junction and Killin.

TIMETABLE 5: BRITISH RAILWAYS TIMETABLE, 1953.

Weekdays only

		am	am	am	pm	pm
Glasgow	dep	4.05	8.00	—	12.12	5.15
Edinburgh	"	—	6.50	—	11.40	4.25
Oban	"	6.05	—	9.18	12.05	4.45
Killin Jct	arr	8.12	10.28	11.20	2.50	7.40
Killin	arr	8.26	10.4l	11.33	3.03	7.54

		am	am	am	pm	pm
Killin	dep	7.42	10.03	10.55	1.42	6.25
Killin Jct	arr	7.55	10.17	11.08	1.56	6.38
Oban	arr	—	12.29	—	4.36	9.27
Edinburgh	"	11.03	—	2.23	4.37	9.58
Glasgow	"	10.23	—	1.30	4.22	9.00

KILLIN JUNCTION and LOCH TAY

Miles				1	2	3	4	5	6	7	8	9	10	11	12	13	14	15
				— WEEK DAYS														
	For continuation of Trains from Junctions see page			Passenger	Mixed	Passenger	Passenger	Mixed	Passenger	Passenger		Passenger	Light Engine	Passenger	Passenger	Passenger	Mixed	
				a.m	a.m	a.m	a.m	p.m	p.m	p.m		p.m	p.m	p.m	p.m	p.m	p.m	
0		Killin Junction	dep	7.10	8.05	10.25	11.13	12.18	2.06	2.47	...	...	5.30	5.30	5.40	6.58	7.40	...
4		Killin	arr	7.22	8.18	10.37	11.25	12.31	2.18	2.59	...	...	5.42	5.42	5.52	7.10	7.53	...
			dep	...	...	...	...	12.55	...	...	...	4.50	...	...	...	...	...	...
5		Loch Tay	arr	...	...	...	...	12.58	...	...	...	4.59	...	...	...	...	...	...
								Commences June 1				Commences June 1	Ceases after May 31	(Not Advertised) Ceases after May 26	Commences June 1	Ceases after May 31		

C.R. TIMETABLES

LOCH TAY and KILLIN JUNCTION

Miles				1	2	3	4	5	6	7	8	9		10	11	12	13	14
				WEEK DAYS														
	For continuation of Trains from Junctions see page			Passenger	Passenger	Mixed	Passenger	Mixed	Mixed	Passenger	Empty Stock	Light Engine		Passenger	Passenger	Passenger	Passenger	
				a.m	a.m	a.m	a.m	a.m	p.m	p.m	p.m	p.m		p.m	p.m	p.m	p.m	
0		Loch Tay	dep	...	...	...	...	...	1.20	...	...	...	...	5.10	...	...	...	...
1		Killin	arr	...	...	...	...	...	1.23	...	...	...	...	5.13	...	...	...	...
			dep	6.43	7.45	10.00	10.55	11.50	1.42	2.25	3.08	3.08	...	5.14	6.39	7.00	7.17	...
5		Killin Junction	arr	6.56	7.58	10.14	11.08	12.04	1.56	2.38	3.21	3.21	...	5.27	6.52	7.13	7.30	...
								Commences June 1	Commences June 1		Ceases after May 26	Ceases after May 31		Commences June 1	Ceases after May 31		Ceases after May 31	

ACKNOWLEDGEMENTS

Mr J.M. Anderson, Killin. (Ex-surfaceman)

Mrs E. Sinclair, Killin. (Ex-signal woman at Killin Junction)

Mrs J.E. Jones. (Close relative of ex-fireman)

Mr C. Hoare. (Present owner of Killin Junction cottages)

Mr N. Carter. Mrs M. O'Donnell. Mr D. Fraser. Mr R. Kay. Mr J. Lambie. Mr C. Neild. Mr G. Williams.

Mr T. Jenkins, Ailsa-Perth Shipbuilders, Troon.

Scottish Records Office, West Register House, Edinburgh.

Mr P. Waylett and Mr G. Earl whose photographs appear with kind permission.

BIBLIOGRAPHY

Anderson, W.J.V.	*The West Highland Railways, A Railway World Special.* Ian Allan, Weybridge.
Cross, Derek	*Steam in Scotland.* Ian Allan, Weybridge.
Kernahan, Jack,	*Steam in the West Highlands.* Bradford Barton. Truro, 1978.
O'Hara, George C.	*Scottish Urban & Rural Branch Lines.* Eroxop. Prestwick, 1986.
Thomas, John	*The Callander to Oban Railway.* David & Charles. Devon, 1965 .
Thomas, John	*A Regional History of the Railways of Great Britain, North of Scotland.* David & Charles, Devon, 1989.

NEWSPAPERS AND JOURNALS

Back Track	Spring 1989 (33-38) M. Roughley.
Courier & Advertiser	September 28, 1965.
Railway Modeller	October 1966 (310).
Railway World	August 1987 (471-473) D. Raynsford.
Steam Railway	July 1986 (23-30) J. Goss.

INDEX